Drawing for Beginners

A Complete Step by Step Guide on How to Draw

Copyrighted@2023

Harriet Roberts

Table of Contents

Chapter One

Drawing Techniques

Learning to draw can seem difficult, especially when you consider the impressive works of art created by experienced illustrators. It's critical to keep in mind that even the greatest artists in history were once beginners. Start by honing some fundamental drawing skills. After that, try drawing more challenging images to depict things like nature, animals, and humans. You'll be astonished at how rapidly your drawing abilities advance if you persevere.

Things to Be Aware Of

• Prior to learning how to shade a shape and add depth, practice drawing simple lines.

• Use perspective and shadows to give your drawings more depth.

• Make use of model images. Drawing a reference point is far simpler than creating anything entirely from scratch.

• Attempt sketching what you observe around you to hone your abilities and perfect your techniques.

Procedure 1:

Basic Drawing Methods

Become comfortable drawing simple curves and lines.

Start by tracing a straight line with the pencil if you're just learning to draw. Much difficult than it appears. To find the most comfortable position, experiment holding your hand at various angles. After you are confident drawing straight lines, try practicing sketching curves by twisting your wrist as you draw.

• On the paper, try tracing a series of thick loops, then a layer of tiny swirls. By doing this, you can increase your coordination on the page.

• Try out different line widths, densities, and textures. Trace zigzagging, wavy, squiggly, and tangled lines if you can.

• After becoming comfortable with lines and curves, try drawing shapes. Consider attempting to fit circles, squares, triangles, or any other two-dimensional shape into a page.

• Get a set of graphite pencils with various hardness if you'd want to experiment.

Depth can be added to a shape by adding shading.

Create a fictional source of light and a simple form like a circle on your page. You should lightly shade with a pencil the areas that are farthest from your light source, leaving the area that is closest to the light source un-shaded. The object's darkest sections should gradually give way to its lightest, closest-to-the-light source, regions as you add more shade.

• Imagine that a lamp is shining downward from the page's upper left corner. Then whatever shape you drew would have no shading in the top-left corner.

• To soften your shadows, try blending them with your finger, an eraser, or a towel.

• Try to master cross-hatching and stippling when you're ready to study more complex shading techniques.

Use cast shadows to give an object a sense of actuality.

After visualizing your light source, create a shadow on the side of the item that is not facing the light source. Though it could be longer or shorter than the thing itself depending on how close or far the light source is, keep the shadow the same shape as the object.

• If you place a bowl of fruit on a table, the bowl will throw a shadow inside the bowl, the table will cast a shadow on the floor, and so will the fruit.

• To make the shadow look more lifelike, blur the edges with your finger or an eraser.

If you require assistance with proportions, draw a grid on the page.

If you're drawing something from a source image, draw multiple evenly spaced vertical and horizontal lines on your paper to form a grid. The identical lines on your source image after that. Examine each square on the illustration, and then duplicate it into the corresponding square on your paper. The final image you create will match the original in size.

• To create a 4 by 3 grid, for instance, you might draw 3 vertical lines and 2 horizontal lines.

• The size of the squares on your paper and your source image can differ. You will invariably change the size as you copy the image you see in each grid.

Using perspective, demonstrate the dimensions of an object.

To start practicing perspective, draw a horizontal line across your paper to represent the horizon. Make a tiny dot along the path. You are now going to vanish. Create two lines that meet at the vanishing point at the bottom of your page. This might substitute for a waterway or a street. The broadest part of the path near the bottom of the page will seem to be closest to you, while the vanishing point will seem to be extremely far away.

• In terms of perspective, closer items appear to be larger than farther away objects.

• More intricate drawings may have two or even three vanishing points, whereas simpler drawings only have one.

• Realistic shading and cast shadows result from an understanding of perspective.

• Draw 3D boxes from various angles to get a feel for how this interacts with other things.

Combine different forms to create more intricate creations.

You can break down more complex items into simpler shapes to draw them once you've mastered the fundamentals of drawing and coloring forms. If you want to draw a person, an automobile, or your hand, have a look at it. Draw the basic elements that make it up. You can practice by drawing the different shapes directly on any image to use as a template.

• Take a photo of an automobile, for instance, and draw the tires' circles, the windshield's rectangle, and other details.

• Add shading to give the shapes that will make up your image dimension once you've roughed them out.

• To make your drawing appear more professional, join the various shapes together with lines to produce a cohesive whole. Remove the outlines when you are done.

Tip

To practice drawing objects, use a mirror. Looks examine your drawing's reflection while holding a mirror in front of it. You'll get a new viewpoint and a fresh look from the reversed image, which might help you learn how to draw more imaginatively all around.

Try drawing contours to get better at internalizing shapes.

Drawing contours helps you develop the ability to create detailed, lifelike outlines. Choose an object to draw, and while you draw it, use your eye to trace the object's outline. Try to keep your eyes as much as you can on the object you are sketching rather than on the hand that is drawing.

• If the drawing isn't flawless, don't stress about it. Simply try to transfer the broad outline of whatever you're viewing on the paper. Do a continuous contour drawing as a game; try to connect all the outlines of what you see without taking your hand off the paper or going over what you've already sketched.

Start by outlining each sketch, and then add details at the end.

Don't immediately worry about the minor details. The basic forms and values should be filled in first, followed by the cleaning up and addition of details. Early focus on tiny details raises the risk of distorting the composition by making one region of your drawing excessively huge or small.

• For example, if you're sketching a flower, you might start by tracing the outline of the petals and stem.

Once it's finished, you might start adding specifics like the flower's center and the arcs of its petals and leaves. The next step would be to add shading and any last-minute touches.

Procedure 2:

Persons and Faces.

To sketch a person's face up close, draw a wide oval and a cross.

Create an upside-down egg with a slightly different-sized top and bottom. Then, softly sketch a line that runs vertically and horizontally through the oval to help you balance the face's proportions. As you don't want them to appear in the final image, only barely sketch them in.

Use the lines to make a crude depiction of the person's face.

Draw the person's eyes along the horizontal line, placing the nose roughly halfway between the eyes and the bottom of the chin. After adding the ears, make sure that the tops of each ear match the eyebrows and the bottoms of the ears meet the nose. Begin by drawing eyebrows above the eyes. A line drawn from the chin to the base of the nose should be placed above the mouth.

• The person's eyelashes, pupils, and hair can all be added later on along with shading and other characteristics.

• Once you're done, remove the vertical and horizontal lines.

Put a circle on top of a trapezoid to make the silhouette of the head.

When drawing someone from a distance, the image will look more realistic if you create the outline of a skull. To do this, first draw a circle, then a brief horizontal line just beneath the circle. You can make the jaw line by drawing angled lines from the circle's sides that drop and meet the horizontal line.

• Men frequently have a wider jaw line than women,

• You can still employ the crossed directional lines from a close-up drawing these lines softly so they don't appear in your final design since they will help you maintain proportion when you fill in the details of the person's face.

Draw a rounded rectangle and an oval to form the human's core.

Just below the head, create a long rectangle that will represent the person's torso. Make the rectangle very small if the person is thin, and wider if they are large. Create a horizontal oval on top of the rectangle's base next. These are the hips of the person.

• Draw a thin rectangle from the subject's head to their core if their neck will be seen in the image.

• Make the rectangle exactly straight if the subject is still. Tilt the rectangle slightly if they're leaning slightly.

Use circles and straight lines to represent the person's limbs.

The top and lower arms, legs, and other body parts of the human should all be depicted by straight lines. the subject's shoulders, knees, elbows, and wrists, as well as any other flexible areas of their body with little circles.

• Draw the circles and lines gently; they are only there to aid in your ability to picture the person's form. You'll take them out when you've added detail to the drawing.

Once the body is roughed out, add clothing, limbs, and other elements.

Prepare to add some detail once you've sketched the person's outline. Fill out the face if you haven't already. Create the limbs, and then remove the lines and circles from the joints. Provide other details like hair, attire, and hands.

• Keep in mind that the less specific you need to be, the further away a person is, so don't be afraid to be creative or expressive here. If you're drawing a huge group of people, concentrate on the outlines.

To capture the spirit of poses and actions, try drawing gestures.

A gesture drawing is a straightforward sketch that depicts motion and form. Starting with a few simple lines, swiftly sketch the shapes and motions you see for no more than 30 to 60 seconds. Keep your lines fluid, twisted, and sketchy. The objective is to create something that appears dynamic and natural rather than clean and polished.

• If you're drawing a human figure, consider drawing a line down the middle of it, from the top of the head to the foot that is supporting the weight.

• Create the rest of the figure around it, adding more lines to represent the hips' and shoulders' angles.

• Focus on keeping your hand moving rather than on accuracy or fine details.

Procedure 3

Landscapes

If you're outside, use your view or a reference image.

Look for a picture of a beautiful natural scene online, or draw what you see when you peek out the window. It's frequently good to have some kind of reference while drawing a landscape to help you get your proportions correct, especially when you're initially starting out.

• Try bringing a sketchbook to a local natural place like a national park or animal refuge if you can't find a photo you like and your home doesn't have a decent view.

To represent the horizon, draw a flat line across your paper.

The horizon line in a landscape photograph is the line that separates the sky and the earth. Wherever you want the horizon to terminate, draw a thin line. Keep in mind that if your horizon has mountains, treetops, buildings, or other high elements, it may not be precisely straight.

• If you position the horizon line a third of the way up from the bottom of the page, your image will be more visually appealing and follow the rule of thirds.

• The viewer will see more of the ground if you draw your horizon higher on the page, and more of the sky if you draw it lower.

Give your image a focus point, like a tree.

Use some attention-grabbing elements for the viewer to look at in your landscape drawing to make it seem more intriguing. This may be a bench, a person, a tree, a structure, and some unusual rocks next to a stream, a barn, a waterfall, or anything else you can think of.

• The largest feature in a painting serves as the focus point most often, but it can also be an object that sticks out due to its color or contrast.

• For instance, if the rest of the colors are boring, a small patch of bright yellow flowers at the base of a stream will probably capture the viewer's attention.

• Search for a model photograph or a scene with a naturally occurring focus point. For instance, your reference image might show a sizable, mature tree.

Keep your proportions consistent by using perspective.

Consider a vanishing point along your horizon line as you draw. Orient every line in your image back to this location. Make the foreground elements larger so they appear closer to the viewer and the background ones smaller.

• For example, if you're drawing trees, you can extend the tops and bottoms of the foreground trees all the way to the paper's edge if you prefer.

• But as the trees go into the background, align the tops and bottoms with an imaginary diagonal that points in the direction of the vanishing point.

Add texture and simplify the details in your drawing.

Don't strive to depict every leaf on a tree, blade of grass, or brick on a paved road while you're drawing a landscape. Instead, outline an object's general shape before including details in discrete areas to give the viewer a sense of texture and movement.

• For instance, to depict a fir tree covered in needles, you might draw a few slender lines.

• Depending on your drawing style, different levels of detail are appropriate. Be free to experiment with the quantity you want to add based on how you are feeling.

Procedure 4

Fun Drawing Activities

Try your hand at drawing a few straightforward objects for still lives.

A bowl of fruit, an arrangement of flowers, or a vase is good places to start. To create a powerful light source, use a lamp. Draw the general shapes of what you see, then add shadows and inner details.

• Sketch what you see rather than how you think the objects ought to look. It's more difficult than it appears.

• These are still-life drawings, and students frequently utilize them in art classes to hone their skills.

Try your hand at cartoons if you have a creative drawing style.

Cartoon drawings are typically simpler than realistic drawings, but they also provide you more creative freedom. For example, you might create a cartoon animal that goes on adventures or you could portray yourself as a superhero. You might also practice drawing a pre-made character, such as your preferred anime or comic book character.

• Pay attention to your main character first, then develop various settings, supporting actors, and things that your cartoon may interact with.

• Experiment with your character's posture and facial expressions to communicate various emotions and actions.

• You can also use your imagination to depict fantastical scenes that appear realistic. If you have a really distinct vision of a dragon in your mind, you might attempt drawing one.

To practice detailing, create an image of your preferred animal.

When you begin to sketch an animal, find a reference photo of one you like and get familiar with its traits. Afterward, begin by sketching the animal's general outline. Draw in any distinctive features, such as the creature's face, wings, or fins, when you're done. Once it is done, gradually add shade and detail until you are happy with the result.

• Animal drawings can be challenging. If you want your picture to look realistic, pay great attention to light and shadows, or if you prefer a cartoonish drawing, put more focus on the animal's distinguishing characteristics.

Chapter Two

Two Simple Techniques for Drawing a Human

One of the numerous talents an artist may have is the ability to draw people. Although though every artist has a unique style of sketching, in order to get started, they all had to understand a few fundamental concepts. There are some easy techniques you may use to sketch the fundamental contour of a person, whether you want to draw a realistic human or a cartoon. You can follow this step-by-step guide to learn the very basics of drawing people.

Important Information

• To draw a realistic figure, first divide your paper into two equal columns of eight rows each. Assign one spot to each body part.

• While sketching a cartoon character, sketch each body part in the correct proportions using simple shapes like circles, squares, and rectangles.

• Once you've connected the pieces of your basic outline, fill in the details by adding things like a face, hair, clothes, and accessories.

• Remove any guide lines, and then add shade to your person to give it more depth and realism.

Procedure 1:

Drawing a Realistic Person

Make an 8-section vertical line by dividing it into equal halves.

One head length, or the length of your person's head from top to bottom, shall be the unit of measurement for each segment. Adult figures are typically 8 head lengths tall, so noting this on your paper at the outset will help you maintain the proper proportions in your design.

The top horizontal line should represent the top of your person's head, and the bottom horizontal line should represent the bottom of your person's feet. Draw horizontal lines to divide the vertical line.

• Since children are often shorter than adults, divide the vertical line into fewer head lengths when drawing a youngster. Use 3 head lengths, for instance, for a toddler, and 6 for a child who is 10 years old.

Draw broad strokes for the body's various organs.

Use the reference lines to aid you with proportions as you lightly sketch the initial shapes of your person's physique. Add broad sketches of the body, arms, legs, and head. The forms don't need to be perfect just yet because this is only a basic sketch.

• The top head length section should include the head's outline.

• The outlines of the person's body and arms should begin in the second head-length portion and stretch all the way down to the fourth section.

• While the outlines of the person's legs should occupy the bottom four head-length sections.

Refine and connect the body's component parts' contours.

To connect the various outlines so they flow together naturally, trace around the body's outside edges. Start tweaking the body's proportions at this stage to make it appear more masculine or feminine, depending on the style you're striving for.

• To depict a manly figure, widen the shoulders, chest, and waist while simultaneously taking in the hips to make them thinner. As you define the outline of your drawing, generally utilize more angular lines.

• To depict someone with feminine features, make the hips and thighs wider and the shoulders and chest area narrower. To highlight your form, use softer, rounder lines.

Include minor particulars such as the hands and facial features.

Draw the knees, hair, and feet in outline. Add breasts and shape the hips and thighs if you're drawing a woman or someone else with feminine features.

• At this time, the person's physique should be done. Define the muscles on the stomach, chest, and arms for a person with masculine features.

Cover the person's body with clothing.

With this part, be imaginative. Draw several shirts, jeans, shoes, and accessories in various cuts and styles. Draw a dress or a skirt over your form for a more feminine appearance. Simply sketch the clothing where it would ordinarily appear on the subject's body if they were wearing it. Then, since such places would be hidden by the clothing, remove any body parts that are inside the lines of the garments.

Remove any unused shading and lines from your drawing.

Go back and remove the horizontal and vertical lines you made to indicate the head length portions at the beginning. Any earlier outline sketches that don't belong in the finished drawing should likewise be removed. After you're done, shade the person's skin, hair, and clothing to give them a more realistic and three-dimensional appearance.

• Pretend there is an imagined light source beaming on one side of your person as you shade your drawing. Then, since the shadows would be on the opposite side of the person's body, shade that area of the body darker.

Procedure 2:

Drawing a Cartoon Person

Make an oval, and then cut it into four equal halves.

The head of your cartoon character will be this. As cartoons typically have exaggerated dimensions, make the head larger than you would for a realistic-looking human. Divide the oval into four equal segments using a horizontal and vertical line.

• The oval's horizontal and vertical lines will be useful when you subsequently draw the cartoon person's face.

Make a rectangle for the body and a cylinder for the neck.

Draw the neck such that it protrudes from the oval's lower center. Finally, to create the body of your cartoon figure, draw a rectangle extending from the base of the neck.

• Make the top of the rectangle narrower and the bottom of the rectangle wider if you want to draw a cartoon character with feminine features.

• If you want to create a cartoon character with masculine features, widen the top and narrow the bottom of the rectangle.

Draw circles for the knees and elbows and cylinders for the arms and legs.

For the arms and legs, draw 2 cylinders with a circle separating each pair. The joints in your drawing will be indicated by the circles. Depending on what your cartoon character is doing, adjust the position of the arms and legs.

Generally speaking, the legs should extend downward from the bottom and the arms should protrude from the top corners of the torso.

• If you're drawing a male cartoon character, use straight, angular lines; if you're creating a female character, use rounded, soft lines.

Make the hands and feet visible.

At the end of each arm, sketch the outline of a hand. At the end of each leg, trace the outline of a foot. Don't stress about getting them exact. Later on, you can go back and make adjustments.

Face and hair should be drawn.

Draw the lips and nose on the vertical line and the eyes on the horizontal line for the face. Make the eyes larger than the rest of the face features as you're sketching a cartoon and not an actual person. Make the hairline slightly lower than the top of the head while drawing the hair.

• Be imaginative in the hairstyle you select. Draw a simple short haircut for your model, or try long or wavy hair.

On the body of the cartoon character, draw clothing.

It's up to you what kind of clothing you want to draw, just like with the hair. Draw a dress, a skirt, shorts, a shirt with short or long sleeves, or any other type of clothing you like. Draw shoes and any other accessories you want your cartoon person to wear, and don't forget to include clothing.

• Since the body portions of your cartoon figure would be hidden by the clothing, after drawing the garments erase anything that is inside the clothing's outline.

Even out the drawing's lines and remove any extraneous ones.

To join all of the outlines you previously generated, trace all the way around your drawing. After that, go back and remove any lines—including the horizontal and vertical lines on the face— that are contained within that outline.

• Once you've removed every trace of the background lines from your drawing, you're done.

Finished.

Chapter Three

Basic Drawings Ideas

Everyone can learn how to draw with a little amount of practice. While some people are inherently talented at producing lifelike visuals, the most of us need to put in some work to improve our abilities.

Dandelion

Dandelions are bright-looking flowers that are simple to draw because you only need to make a wavy stem, typical leaves, and a fuzzily flower. And the best part is that all you need to get started is a pencil and some paper.

Magnolias

Magnolias are exquisite flowers that come in a variety of hues, including white, pink, and blue. Another well-liked tree for illustrations with a natural subject is the magnolia. While appearing fragile, the magnolia is simple to depict.

Roses

Roses are among the most popular flowers in the world, so it seems sense that so many people want to include them in their artwork. When the flower is broken down into tiny, straightforward shapes, drawing a rose is simple.

Birds

Birds are an interesting topic for beginning artists since they come in a variety of colors, forms, and sizes.

Cat in the Hat

You can practice drawing well-known cartoon figures, like the Cat in the Hat, once you've mastered the principles of cartoon drawing.

Cartoon Penguins

A penguin is adorable, humorous, and simple to draw using only lines and basic shapes. As a result, drawing a penguin is a great project for amateur artists. Also, if you enjoy adorable cartoonish illustrations,

SpongeBob Squarepants

Children and adults alike love the crazy cartoon character SpongeBob Squarepants. Due to SpongeBob's cartoon character's simplistic drawing style, which is simple to imitate, it's an excellent approach to develop your artistic abilities.

A Lifelike Dragon

Unlike the last dragon drawing for children, this realistic dragon sketch is intended for artists who are prepared to advance to the next level because it contains more intricate elements.

Dinosaurs

When honing your drawing talents, it's a good idea to blend dinosaurs and dragons because they have certain similarities.

Robots

Kids who are interested in technical sketching should consider robots because they can use their own rules and compasses. In addition, it's worthwhile to investigate the various robot versions.

Fruit

Fruit is usually a favorite subject for artists since you may draw inspiration from actual materials rather than just reference photographs. Fruit seems simple to draw, but it can be challenging to capture minute details, such as the dimples on an orange's skin.

Once you have mastered numerous fruits, you can combine them to design a traditional fruit basket or, if you're feeling particularly festive, a cornucopia.

Trees

As no two trees are exactly same, there are numerous methods to depict them.

Leaves

After becoming proficient at drawing trees, you can advance by learning to draw a variety of leaves. For instance, you may use leaves to embellish a flower pot or make a picture with a fall theme.

Cherry Blossoms

Cherry blossoms are lovely trees with distinctively shaped pink or white petals. For romantic sceneries or springtime vistas, cherry blossoms are great.

Sceneries from Nature

Once you've mastered drawing trees and their features, such as cherry blossoms and leaves, you may combine them all to produce a full-fledged natural landscape. Nature scenes come in all different sizes and shapes, but they all have a horizon line.

The Sky and Clouds

It can be tedious to draw a landscape with a sky and clouds because you are likely to make mistakes.

Beach

Sketching a beach requires mastering a variety of aspects, including the sky and sun, water, the reflection of the sky in the water, sand, and tropical trees. If you want to draw a beach in a more straightforward manner.

Snowflakes

Because they are distinct and symmetrical, snowflakes are a great subject to practice sketching with a pencil and a ruler.

Mandalas

Mandalas are distinctive and symmetrical, like snowflakes;

therefore you should try sketching one if you want to practice creating intricate patterns using different shapes and symbols.

Houses

Due to their straightforward design and characteristics, houses are among the first objects you learn to draw in kindergarten.

Cars

In addition to learning how to sketch houses, toddlers also learn how to draw cars. It's best to start with 2D automobiles if you want to improve your artistic abilities to design 3D cars.

Spacecraft

The only aspect of spaceships that is possibly unrelated to rocket science is drawing a spaceship.

If you enjoy science fiction, you've probably had at least one dream in which you were piloting one of these powerful machines.

Angel Wing

If you enjoy drawing angels and devils or if you want to become a tattoo artist, angel wings are a terrific subject to draw. While drawing angel wings, it's crucial to get the proportions right.

Dimensions of the Human Body

The proportions of the human body, such as the height and waist of the individual, must be grasped in order to learn how to draw human bodies accurately. You can begin to map out where each body part should be in relation to the others after you have these fundamental measurements.

Body of Men and Women

You might begin investigating the distinctions between male and

female body types and sketch
them after learning about human
body dimensions.

When drawing a male and female
form, you'll notice a big
difference.

The Size of Your Face

There is no one method that
works for everyone when it
comes to drawing facial
proportions. To figure out what
works the best for you, you might
need to explore a little.

Eyes

While drawing eyes is one of the
most difficult components of
painting a portrait, it's also one of

the most crucial. A painting's eyes have the power to make or destroy it since they are the portals to the soul. Fortunately, there are a few easy techniques you may use to create expressive and realistic eyes in your paintings.

Mouth

Although it may appear difficult, with a little effort, it is possible to accurately depict the subtleties of this facial feature.

Teeth

The teeth are one of the trickiest parts to draw correctly, as anyone who has attempted to sketch a mouth will attest to. Teeth are not only tiny and complicated, but they also have a significant impact on the facial expression.

Straight Hair

Drawing straight hair can be difficult, but with experience, it's definitely doable.

Underwater Hair

Understanding how light works in water is essential for painting underwater hair. The fundamental idea is that light is refracted when it goes through water, but you'll need to practice a little to get the hang of it. As a result, it bends, which is what provides the impression that submerged hair is afloat in the water.

Faces of Men and Women

Drawing male and female features can be challenging since they have so many delicate nuances that must be captured in order to produce a lifelike image. To become familiar with the proportions of the various features, such as the eyes, mouths, and teeth, for instance, you must study the structure of the face. Then, it's essential to understand how male and female faces differ.

Anime Eyes

Anime eyes are big, expressive, and frequently the most distinguishing characteristic of a character. Even while drawing anime eyes might initially seem difficult, anyone can master the skill with a little practice.

Anime Hair

After their eyes, anime characters' hair is perhaps what makes them stand out from other cartoon characters. In anime, hair is frequently depicted with exaggerated curls and spikes that are impossible to create in real life.

The Bodies of Anime Men and Women

Drawing the bodies of anime's male and female characters can be enjoyable and gratifying. Male and female bodies share some similarities, but there are also significant distinctions. As an illustration, male anime characters frequently have wider shoulders and chests than female characters, which typically have narrower hips and waists.

The Deadpool

A great comic book character to practice your nascent artistic abilities with is Deadpool. You don't have to bother about sketching minute details like eyes or hair because he wears a full-body suit that totally conceals the head.

Caricatures

Caricatures are humorous drawings that exaggerate the subject's physical characteristics. For a fun and original way to amuse your friends and family, consider learning how to draw caricatures. The best way to get started is to practice on a willing friend or yourself.

A Glass of Water

One of the easiest and most adaptable objects to draw is a glass of water. Whether you're trying to catch the light on a still life or quickly sketching a portrait, a glass of water may add interest and complexity to your drawing.

Drawing Methods for Shading

Anyone who wants to be an artist must learn how to shade. Drawings gain depth and character with shading, which may also be used to produce a variety of effects, from delicate highlights to strong shadows. While learning how to shade may initially seem difficult, it's actually pretty simple if you start with basic shapes and subsequently advance your knowledge.

Conclusion

The idea of starting from scratch while drawing something intimidates many individuals. Yet anyone can learn to draw rather effectively with a little perseverance, practice, and examples. So if your initial attempts fall short of expectations, don't give up. You'll be astonished at how rapidly your talents advance if you make it a priority to work on your drawings daily.

www.ingramcontent.com/pod-product-compliance
Lightning Source LLC
Chambersburg PA
CBHW071140220526
45467CB00015B/1662